# C++

## *Programming Basics for Absolute Beginners*

## Nathan Clark

Any trademarks which are used are done so without consent and any use of the same does not imply consent or permission was gained from the owner. Any trademarks or brands found within are purely used for clarification purposes and no owners are in anyway affiliated with this work.

# Books in this Series

C++: Programming Basics for Absolute Beginners

C++: A Detailed Approach to Practical Coding

# Table of Contents

Introduction ------------------------------------------------------------- 1

1. What is C++? ----------------------------------------------------- 3

2. Basic Rules ------------------------------------------------------27

3. C++ Sample Library --------------------------------------------45

4. Capabilities of C++ ---------------------------------------------59

5. Limitations of C++ ---------------------------------------------63

6. Practical Application of C++ ----------------------------------67

7. Making Your First C++ Program ----------------------------69

8. How to Avoid Adding Bugs to Your Programs -------------79

9. How to Avoid Being Hacked --------------------------------- 83

10. Glossary of Terms --------------------------------------------87

Conclusion--------------------------------------------------------101

# Introduction

Welcome to the wonderful world of programming, the chapters contained in this book will give you a basic understanding of programming in C++. By its final chapter you will be able to create a complete program on your own, using C++.

In order to use the information contained in this book, you must have a computer that runs Windows, Macintosh, Linux, or UNIX operating system. You must know how to run a program, copy a file, create a folder, and navigate through menus. These are the only requirements for being able to program using C++.

Thank you for your interest in this versatile language and let's have some fun!

# 1. What is C++?

Programming is simply organizing data and instructions in a sequence. This is called "monolithic programming."

It is a sequential set of instructions used to solve a singular problem. Execution is made using statements. C++ can be used to program almost anything, in that respect, it is practical for every programmer to have a basic understanding of this language. A great way to highlight its practicality is to compare it to its father language, C:

- C is known as a structured programming language making it sometimes difficult to keep things in line once you run the program.

- C++ follows the newer programming language ideas and is object oriented.

- C does not have inline functions.

- C++ does support inline function.

- C does not support functions with default arguments.

- C++ does support functions with default arguments.

- C does not have exception handling.

- C++ does support exception handling.

- C only utilizes pointers.

- C++ utilizes pointers and references.

- C is a mid-level language.

- C++ is a high-level language with qualities that can be applied to low and mid-level languages.

- C does not secure data.

- C++ hides data that can't be accessed by external functions.

Let's have a closer look at object oriented programming. Although the name seems straightforward, the concepts behind it might not be.

# 1.1 What is Object Oriented Programming?

Object oriented programming, often referred to as OOP (for the sake of brevity) is summarized by two very simple principles. These are "classification" and "abstraction". If we break these two terms up, we can quickly understand the underlying features of C++ being an object-oriented programming language.

Abstraction can be thought of as the art of assumption. Take a television for instance, we don't need to know exactly how the inside of the television works for us to be able to operate it. We assume that by pressing the "on" button, that the television will follow our command and turn on.

This is essentially what abstraction is. We know that by pressing the "on" button, the television will not do anything other than what is expected. In this case, the button we press represents the interface we are dealing with. Each subsequent instruction we send to the television works exactly the same way, and we assume that it will follow these commands without disobeying.

Classification is identifying what the object we are dealing with is. If we asked ourselves, "what is a television?" we would say it is an appliance used in our living rooms. If we asked what a living room appliance was, we would say it is an entertainment appliance. The television is an instance of the class "living room." The class "living room" is a subclass of "entertainment." Classification is a means to reduce the amount of information that we have to remember.

C++ is a language that is used for general purposes that supports practical, object-oriented, and generic programming. The C++ language is basically a modern version of the original C language developed in the early 1970s. It was subsequently redeveloped into C++ by Bjarne Stroustrup in 1979, making it the preferred programming language of the time.

C++ is a mid-level programming language in that it can be used for both simple programs and very advanced programs alike. The language can be used for high-performance applications like web servers and operating systems, and can even be found in many modern game engines.

To make a code into a program, the programmer must compile and convert the code into an executable file that the computer can run. This is appropriately termed "compiling".

## 1.2 What is a Compiler?

At its core, a computer only works in one language. This language is called binary language, meaning that the computer only reads instructions in sequences of 0's and 1's.

This is what that language could look like for a single instruction.

```
00000 - 10011110
```

As an example, the binary code instruction below allows a user to input two numbers, the computer then adds those two numbers together and shows the total. The instruction would look like this:

```
00000 – 10011110

00001 – 11110100

00010 – 10011110

00011 – 11010100

00100 – 10111111

00101 – 00000000
```

Fortunately, to make programming easier, high-level programming languages were invented that makes programming much less tedious and less error prone. This is where C++ comes in. An example of what a comparable C++ code looks like is shown below:

```
int a, b, sum;

cin >> a;

cin >> b;

sum = a + b;
```

Don't be concerned about the code itself, but notice that it is far simpler than the binary code shown above. Both codes shown execute the exact same goal.

Because computers only understand binary, and we humans use high-level languages such as C++, we must translate the language into binary before the program can be executed. This is accomplished through a special program called a compiler. C++ was created to be a compiled language.

This essentially means that the language can be directly translated to binary by the systems built into numerous programming applications. In order for C++ to be directly translated however, a specific set of tools are required. These are the compiler and its linker.

Because C++ is so strong and has a good compiler, it is going to be one of the most used programming languages around. It has a lot of practical uses that makes it even more popular, and you will be able to learn the language quickly and efficiently.

Keep in mind that C++ is used to make programming easier as a directly translatable programming language. There are many compilers available to use. Here is a list of some of the most commonly used programs:

- C++Builder
- Turbo C++ (for explorer)
- C++ Compiler
- CINT
- Borland C++
- Turbo C++ (for DOS)
- Clang
- CodeWarrior
- Comeau
- CoSy Compiler Development System
- Digital Mars
- EDGE ARM
- Edison Design Group
- GCC
- HP aC++
- IAR C/C++ Compiler
- Intel C++ Compiler
- KAI C++ Compiler
- Microtec
- MULTI
- Open Watcom
- Open64
- PathScale

There are many more, and most of these compilers will be available for the average windows operating system computer with a few exceptions.

## 1.3 Sample Applications

Below are some of the aspects you can achieve with C++ programs. In addition to the type of programs you can develop, a small program snippet is shown.

Don't be too concerned with understanding the code of the program snippets right away, we will get into much greater detail of each topic in later chapters in the series. If you have some programming knowledge, the program snippets will give you an idea of how the topics are handled within C++.

# 1.3.1 System Software

This is a program that has been designed to run with the application programs and hardware of the computer. It is often the interface that shows up between these two.

## *Example 1: The following program is used to showcase a program that works with a Windows based system.*

```cpp
#include <windows.h>
#include <iostream>

using namespace std;

// The thread will call this function
DWORD WINAPI Display(LPVOID lpParameter) {
    cout<<"Creating thread"<<endl;

}


int main () {

// We want to start 10 threads


    for (int i = 0; i < 10; i++) {
```

```
    DWORD myThreadID;

    HANDLE myHandle = CreateThread(0, 0, Display, 0, 0,
&myThreadID);
cout<<myThreadID<<endl;


  }
}
```

The above program is a good way to show how to develop
systems software with C++. In the above example, we are just
writing a program which makes use of threads in C++. All
operating systems nowadays work on the basis of threads and
hence it makes sense for the programming language to also
work with threads. We will be looking at threads in much
more detail in Book 3 of the series.


# 1.3.2 Client-Server Applications

This refers to a distributed application structure that divides
tasks between the servers and clients. Servers are the
benefactors of a service or resource, and clients are the service
supplicants.

The below example shows the best way to create server based
components using a concept known as classes. We will see
classes in much more detail in Book 2 of the series. But with
the help of classes you can create server components which
clients can make use of.

## Example 2: The following program is used to showcase the best way to create server side components.

```cpp
#include <iostream>
using namespace std;

// Defining the student class
class Student
{
public:
// The members of the class
   int studentID;

   string studentName;
};

int main () {

// variable of the type student
Student stud1;

   stud1.studentID=1;

   stud1.studentName="John";

cout<<"Student ID "<<stud1.studentID<<endl;

cout<<"Student Name "<<stud1.studentName;

   return 0;
}
```

So in the above example we are creating a class of the type Student.

We then have properties which define the class such as Name and ID and methods which are used to work with the properties of the class.

# 1.3.3 Embedded Firmware

This refers to a memory chip that stores specialized software designed to control embedded device functions.

Embedded is a term used in this scenario to describe a function taking place as part of a larger system.

A lot of embedded systems will use artificial intelligence which is based off regular expressions. C++ also has support for regular expressions. The below program shows an example of regular expressions, which we will look into more detail in Book 3 of the series.

## *Example 3: The following program is used to showcase how to use regular expressions in C++.*

```cpp
#include <iostream>
#include <string>
#include <regex>

using namespace std;

int main () {

  if (regex_match("Hello World", regex("(Hello)(.*)")))
    cout << "Match found";
}
```

The above program checks whether the keyword of 'Hello' is present in the string based on regular expressions.

## 1.3.4 Drivers

This refers to a program that controls a device, such as printers, disk drives, or keyboards. A lot of device driver programs will use simple logic algorithms which are also present in C++.

For example, if you look at printers, they can be based on queue logic. All the print jobs will be sent to the job queue. In C++, there are classes which help in these simple algorithms. The below example shows how to use queues in C++. We will discuss more about queues in the algorithm chapter, in Book 3 of the series.

***Example 4: The following program is used to showcase how to use queues in C++.***

```
#include <iostream>
#include <queue>

using namespace std;

int main ()

{
    std::queue<int> Example;

    Example.push(1);
    Example.push(2);
    Example.push(3);

    cout<<"Is the queue empty " <<Example.empty()<<endl;
}
```

The above program is used to create a queue and add 3 elements to the queue. Finally the program also checks if the queue is empty or not.

There are six essential concepts that help to make the C++ system work well. These six concepts are:

# 1.3.5 Polymorphism

This refers to a feature of a programming language that allows routines to use variables of differing types at differing times. The code below shows a simple example of polymorphism. We will be looking into more detail of polymorphism in Book 3 of the series. Polymorphism helps in creating base and derived classes and then base objects from either class type.

## *Example 5: The following program is used to showcase a simple example of polymorphism.*

```
#include <iostream>
using namespace std;

class Person

{
public:
    int ID;

    string Name;

    void Display()
    {
        cout<<"ID "<<ID<<endl;
```

```cpp
      cout<<"Name "<<Name;

  }
  void InputName(string pName)
  {
    Name=pName;
  }
};



class Student:public Person {
public:
  void InputName(string pName)
  {
    Name=pName;
  }
  void Display()
  {
    cout<<"Student ID "<<ID<<endl;

    cout<<"Student Name "<<Name<<endl;

  }
};
int main () {

  Student stud1;

  stud1.ID=1;

  stud1.InputName("John");

  stud1.Display();

  Person per1;
```

```
per1.ID=2;

per1.InputName("Mark");

per1.Display();

return 0;
}
```

# 1.3.6 Virtual Functions

This is a function that can be redefined in a derived class. When you refer to a derived class object using a pointer or a reference to the base class, you can call a virtual function for that object and execute the derived class's version of the function.

We will look into more detail of virtual functions in Book 2 of the series. But for now, we are showing a simple example of how virtual functions can be implemented.

### *Example 6: The following program is used to showcase virtual functions.*

```
#include <iostream>
using namespace std;

class Person

{
public:
    int ID;

    string Name;
```

```cpp
  void virtual Display()
  {
    cout<<"ID "<<ID<<endl;

    cout<<"Name "<<Name;

  }
  void InputName(string pName)
  {
    Name=pName;
  }
};


class Student:public Person {
public:
  void InputName(string pName)
  {
    Name=pName;
  }
  void Display()
  {
    cout<<"Student ID "<<ID<<endl;

    cout<<"Student Name "<<Name<<endl;

  }
};
int main () {

  Student stud1;
  Person *per1;

  stud1.ID=1;

  stud1.InputName("John");
```

```
  stud1.Display();

per1=&stud1;
  per1->Display();

  return 0;
}
```

# 1.3.7 Templates

This is the foundation of generic programming, it is a blueprint for creating a generic function.

We will go into more detail on templates in Book 3 of the series. But for now, we are showing a simple example of how templates can be implemented.

### *Example 7: The following program is used to showcase the way to use templates in functions.*

```
#include <iostream>
using namespace std;

// Here we are defining a template which can accept any generic
type
template <class GenericType>

// Genertic type can be replaced with any generic data type
// The function accepts 2 parameters of the data type
// The function also returns a value of that data type

GenericType MaxValue (GenericType a, GenericType b) {
```

```
// The function has the logic to return the largest of 2 numbers
   return (a>b?a:b);
}

int main () {

   // Here we are calling the function with integer data types


cout<<"The maximum value is "<<MaxValue(1,2);

   return 0;
}
```

# 1.3.8 Pointers

This refers to an object that's value points to another value stored elsewhere in the computer's memory. This is an important concept in C++. We will go into greater detail on pointers in Book 2 of the series. But for now, we are showing a simple example of how pointers can be implemented.

## *Example 8: The following program is used to showcase how to define pointers.*

```
#include <iostream>
using namespace std;


int main () {

   int i;

   i=10;
```

```
cout<<" The value of i is "<<i<<endl;
cout<<" The memory address value of i is "<<&i<<endl;

//defining the pointer
int *p;

p=&i;

cout<<" The value of i is "<<*p<<endl;

}
```

## 1.3.9 Namespaces

Namespaces are used to organize code into logical groups. It is used especially when the code base includes multiple libraries. We will look into more detail of namespaces in Book 3 of the series. But for now, we are showing a simple example of how namespaces can be implemented.

### *Example 9: The following program is used to showcase the way to use namespaces.*

```
#include <iostream>
using namespace std;

// One namespace
namespace NameA{
  void FunctionA(){
    cout << "This is namespace A " << endl;
  }
}

// Second namespace
namespace NameB{
  void FunctionA(){
```

```
      cout << "This is namespace B " << endl;
   }
}

int main () {

   // Calls function from first name space.
   NameA::FunctionA();

   // Calls function from second name space.
   NameB::FunctionA();

   return 0;
}
```

## 1.4 Editors

You can write and compile a program either by using notepad and a compiler or by using something that is known as an integrated development environment or IDE.

## 1.4.1 Using Notepad

Probably the easiest form of development is to type the program in notepad and then use a C++ compiler to compile and run the program. So let's start with the following example of a simple piece of code.

```
#include <iostream>
using namespace std;


   int main () {
      std::cout << "Hello world";
   }
```

The above code is pretty simple and all it does is to display "Hello world" to the user. Now if you had to install a C++ compiler, the GCC being the common compiler used, then you can compile and execute the program as follows:

- First save the above code entered in notepad as a C++ file. Let' say you save the file as example.c.

- Next if you are in Windows, open the command prompt window.

- In command prompt, enter the following command.

```
gcc example.c
```

So here you issue the gcc command and add the file name as the input. You should then get the below output which shows that the program has been compiled successfully and also gets run successfully.

**Hello world**

**Process finished with exit code 0**


# 1.4.2 Using an Integrated Development Environment

Using an integrated development environment has a lot of advantages, because it does tend to make coding much easier.

So for example, if you had to compile and run a C++ program, you would probably just have to click a button and the editor would do the rest.

Some of the other major advantages of having an integrated development environment are given below:

- Smart Editor - Some editors have the facility to analyze the context of your project and help you code faster. Some of them have smart code completion, formatting and helpful views with code insight.

- Easy Navigation - Most editors can help you navigate your way through the code with instant navigation to a symbol, class or file. Inspect the calls or types hierarchy and easily search anywhere for nearly everything.

- Code Generation - You can save time on unnecessary typing since the editor can code-complete many things for you. This includes getters/setters for class methods. You can also use refactoring to improve and clean up your code.

- Code Analysis - Some editors have built-in error handlers to highlight warnings and errors in the code immediately as you type, and also suggest quick-fixes.

- Run and Debug - It becomes easier to run and debug projects in an editor.

- Testing - Some editors also have built-in tools which can be used to add test frameworks which can be used to test your code.

- Source Control - Some editors have built-in tools that support the most popular source code versioning tools such as Subversion, Git, GitHub, Mercurial, CVS, Perforce, and TFS.

Some of the editors available for C++ are:

- Netbeans for C/C++ Development.

- Eclipse CDT(C/C++ Development Tooling)

- CodeLite IDE.

- Bluefish Editor.

- Brackets Code Editor.

- Atom Code Editor.

- Sublime Text Editor.

## 1.5 The Benefits of Using C++

If you are brand new to the world of coding, it may seem somewhat intimidating in the beginning. There are many different components to programming, and several different programming languages available to use.

This can all get confusing when choosing a language to start out with. Let's take a look at some of the benefits and drawbacks that come with using C++. This should provide some guidance when deciding whether C++ is for you, if you are just starting out. On the other hand, if you are not new to programming, it should point out some features that differ from other languages.

## 1.5.1 Advantages

There are numerous advantages to choosing C++. It is fast, efficient and will be the perfect tool to use when just getting started in the world of programming. Some of the advantages include:

- Object oriented: This is a newer form of programming language that makes it easier for someone who is just getting started to enjoy the language. Simply put, it helps to keep things in place and ensures that things don't get lost and cause errors later on.

- Portable: C++ is a programming language that can be used no matter the hardware. You can use any type of computer and any type of operating system, to make it work.

- Low-level language: This makes it easier to learn C++, because it isn't as complex as some of the other programming languages. Nevertheless, it still has a lot of power and functionality behind it.

- General purpose: C++ is a general purpose language, making it easy to learn and perfect for basic coding. It also works well with certain other languages, making it possible to add features and functionality.

- Compatible with C: This makes it easier to use if you intend to combine it with the C language.

- Big library: The library is going to be your best friend when learning how to use C++. It will provide you with code that you can work with, rather than writing it all out.

## 1.5.2 Disadvantages

Despite all the positive aspects of C++, there are a few drawbacks that put it at a disadvantage compared to some of the other languages. Some of the disadvantages include:

- It lacks in security: Because C++ has a pointer, global variables, and friend function; it is not as secure as some of the other languages. This can be an issue for some developers, and you may want to add in some additional security, depending on your usage.

- The library can be locked, depending on your operating system: While the library is a great feature available with most programming languages, C++ is slightly different. You will have a different library based on whether you are using Linux, Windows or Mac and these are locked, making it difficult to bring in more of the codes you need.

- It doesn't support garbage collection: If you need to throw out codes, this is going to be difficult inside of C++.

- No support threads: Your support with this program is going to be pretty limited. The program itself is not going to provide any support, and you may have to go online to find your answers.

- Can be hard to debug: When it comes to the numerous programming languages available, C++ can be hard to debug. This can make it difficult for someone who is new to programming to troubleshoot problems.

# 2. Basic Rules

## 2.1 Before We Begin

Important aspects to consider:

- All programs written in C++ have the extension ".cc".

- Every single line of code has a simple instruction.

- All variables are shown when they are needed individually, not before.

- Variables should be shown in the most visible scope possible.


Average situations that do not call for a variable include:

- When reading.

- When the value of the given variable depends on a condition.

- When the value of the given variable includes a loop.

- When the given variable will be utilized immediately as a return parameter.

## 2.2 Basic C++ Terms

## 2.2.1 Operators

These are the symbols (+ - * < !) that execute intended actions using one or more variables. There are many different types of operators that you can use, including the comparison operator, the arithmetic operator, and more. We go into greater detail on operators in Book 2 of the series. As an introduction, here is an example of operator usage:

### *Example 10: The following program is used to showcase the way to use operators.*

```
#include <iostream>
using namespace std;


  int main () {
    // We are defining 2 variables
    int a=5;
    int b=6;

    // Here we are using the + operator
    int c=a+b;
    std::cout << " The value of c is "<<c;
  }
```

The output of the above program will be as follows:

**The value of c is 11**

The above program is making use of the addition operator to add 2 numbers.

## 2.2.2 Cin

The Cin command is one of the simplest input commands that you can use. An example of cin usage is shown below:

### *Example 11: The following program is used to showcase the way to use a cin function.*

```cpp
#include <iostream>
using namespace std;


  int main () {

    int a;

    cout<<"Please enter a value = ";
    cin>>a;
    std::cout << " The value of a is "<<a;
  }
```

The output of the above program will be as follows:

**Please enter a value =**

**5**
**The value of a is 5**

In the above program we are using the cin command to get a value from the user and then output the same value back to console.

## 2.2.3 If-Statements

An if-statement is going to bring your code to new levels and basically allows the program to make decisions on its own. The below program showcases a simple way to use if statements.

### *Example 12: The following program is used to showcase the way to use an if statement.*

```cpp
#include <iostream>
using namespace std;


  int main () {

    int a=5;

    if(a==5) {
       cout << "The value is 5";
    }

       else
    {
       cout << "The value is not 5";
    }
  }
```

The output of the above program will be as follows:

**The value is 5**

In the above program we are comparing a variable value to 5. If the value is 5 then we tell the user that the value is equal to 5 else not.

## 2.2.4 Test Condition

A test condition is a type of Boolean expression. It is used to help you branch out the implementation of your program. The below program showcases a simple way to use test conditions.

***Example 13: The following program is used to showcase the way to use a test conditions statement.***

```
#include <iostream>
using namespace std;


  int main () {

    int a=1;

    while(a<5) {
      cout << "The value is "<<a<<endl;
      a++;
    }

  }
```

The output of the above program will be as follows:

**The value is 1**

**The value is 2**

**The value is 3**

**The value is 4**

So in the above example we are using the white loop to test the condition for the value of a. As long as the value of a is less than 5, we keep on executing the code in the while loop.

# 2.2.5 Switch-Statement

The switch statement will make it easier to have different results appear in the system based on the value of your variable. Let's look at an example of the switch statement.

*Example 14: The following program is used to showcase the way to use a switch statement.*

```
#include <iostream>
using namespace std;

int main () {

  char a = 'B';

  switch(a) {
    case 'A' :
      cout << "The value is A" << endl;
      break;
    case 'B' :
      cout << "The value is B" << endl;
      break;
    case 'C' :
      cout << "The value is C" << endl;
      break;
    default :
      cout << "Invalid character" << endl;
  }
```

```
    return 0;
}
```

The output of the above program will be as follows:

**The value is B**

In the above program we are using the switch statement to see what the value of the variable a is. If the variable is equal to 'B' then we display the message accordingly.


## 2.2.6 Break

This keyword is utilized if you want the computer program to stop doing the switch statement or the loop right away. Let's see an example of how we can use the break statement.

### *Example 15: The following program is used to showcase the way to use a break statement.*

```
#include <iostream>
using namespace std;

int main () {

    int a=1;
    while(a<5) {
        cout << a;
        a++;
        break;
    }
    return 0;
}
```

The output of the above program will be as follows:

**1**

In the above code we are using the break statement to break away from the while loop.

## 2.2.7 Loop

This is a section of your code that will keep on repeating. This repeats until the code tells it to stop or the condition is no longer true.

### Example 16: The following program is used to showcase the way to use a loop condition.

```
#include <iostream>
using namespace std;


  int main () {

    int a=1;

    while(a<5) {
      cout << "The value is "<<a<<endl;
      a++;
    }


  }
```

The output of the above program will be as follows:

**The value is 1**

**The value is 2**

34

**The value is 3**

**The value is 4**

So in the above example we are using the while loop to test the condition for the value of a. As long as the value of a is less than 5, we keep on executing the code in the while loop.

# 2.2.8 Default

This particular keyword is going to be used to supply code to your switch statement. If none of the other cases in the code match with the switch statement parameters, the default will be run.

*Example 17: The following program is used to showcase the way to use a switch statement.*

```cpp
#include <iostream>
using namespace std;

int main () {

  char a = 'Z';

  switch(a) {
    case 'A' :
      cout << "The value is A" << endl;
      break;
    case 'B' :
      cout << "The value is B" << endl;
      break;
    case 'C' :
      cout << "The value is C" << endl;
```

```
      break;
    default :
      cout << "Invalid character" << endl;
  }

  return 0;
}
```

The output of the above program will be as follows:

**Invalid character**

In the above code we can see that the default condition gets executed because none of the normal conditions satisfy the value of a.

# 2.3 Structure of a Program

Most programs have five parts:

- Inclusions

- Constants

- Types

- Procedures

- Main program

# 2.3.1 Inclusions and Namespaces

Write only absolutely necessary inclusions, always start with #include.

The admitted inclusions comprise of the following:

- <iostream>: can only use the construction
  cin >>variable1>> variable2...;

- To read;
  cout << expression1 << expression2...;

- To write; if you are required to write a real number, then you must choose the number of decimals (d) before the lines of code at the beginning of the main.
  cout.setf(ios::fixed);
  cout.precision(d);

At the end of the line of code, you should write "endl".

## Example 18: The following program is used to showcase the way to use the above conditions.

```
#include <iostream>
using namespace std;

int main () {

  int a = 1;

  cout<<"The value of a is "<<a<<endl;

  return 0;
}
```

In the above program

- We are ensuring the use the include statement for the iostream library.

- We are using the cout statement properly.

- We are adding the endl to the cout expression.

## 2.3.2 Definition of the Constants

This can remain empty. Every constant has to be defined in one line. It should look like this:

- const name_of_type name_of_constant = value;

The key word here is "const", this creates a constant variable. If this is not added, the variable becomes a "forbidden" variable. "Forbidden" variables are, you guessed it, not allowed.

### *Example 19: The following program is used to showcase the way to define constants.*

```
#include <iostream>
using namespace std;

int main () {

  const int a = 1;

  cout<<"The value of a is "<<a<<endl;

  return 0;
}
```

In the above program

- We are defining the variable "a" to be a constant expression.

## 2.3.3 Definition of Types

There are four basic types that can be used, these are:

- int, double, bool, and char.

The use of class to define a new type is not allowed.

### *Example 20: The following program is used to showcase the way to define types.*

```cpp
#include <iostream>
using namespace std;

int main () {

    // defining an integer type
    int a = 1;
    // defining an float type
    float b=1.1;
    // defining an boolean type
    bool c=true;
    // defining an character type
    char d='Z';

    // Displaying the integer type
    cout<<"The value of a is "<<a<<endl;


    // Displaying the float type
    cout<<"The value of b is "<<b<<endl;


    // Displaying the boolean type
    cout<<"The value of c is "<<c<<endl;
```

```
// Displaying the character type
cout<<"The value of d is "<<d<<endl;

return 0;
}
```

In the above program

- We are defining a program to use the different types in C++.


# 2.3.4 Procedures

This can remain empty. There are two kinds of procedures, actions and functions.

- Actions - Do not return anything, this is quantified by void. The most useful way to accomplish this is as follows: input, input/ output, output.

- Functions - Return any kind of type. All parameters are input parameters.

Avoid writing over names by giving functions different names than the name given to the procedure.

### Example 21: The following program is used to showcase the way to use procedures.

```
#include <iostream>
using namespace std;

void Display()
{
    cout<<"Hello World"<<endl;
```

```
}

int DisplayA()
{
  return 1;
}


int main () {

  Display();
  cout<<DisplayA();
  return 0;
}
```

In the above program:

- We are defining a procedure called Display which does not return any value to the calling program.

- And we are defining a procedure called DisplayA which returns an integer to the calling program.


## 2.3.5 Main Program

This part of the process is the most important. (Not to discredit any of the other incredibly important steps). The main is responsible for controlling and running the program, execution of the program begins here.

```
<em>{

cout<<"This is my first program in C++/n";
```

```
getch();

Return 0;

}

</em>
```

- This is a basic example of the body of the main function. The body of any function should be enclosed by braces "{}".

- There are three statements in this example; every statement ends with a semicolon ";".

- The first statement made in this example is a "cout" statement. Cout is an object which relates to the basic output stream and '<<' is the inserted operator.

- The '/n' character is known as an "escape sequence." It shows the next output onto a new line.

- The 'getch()' function takes a single character as input.

- The output screen will remain open until the user presses a key on the keyboard.

- Finally, the 'return 0' statement shows the main returns a value of 0 to the compiler or operating system.

These are the basic rules of C++. It is a lot to take in at first, but it will make more sense as you continue.

Next up, are a few excellent tables to understand many terms associated with the C++ programming language.

The code keys provided are for the "Armadillo" open source linear algebra library for C++. It will provide an easier understanding of the computation needed and help identify key terms used in programming with C++.

# 3. C++ Sample Library

This information is provided for reference, do not feel as though you are required to memorize any of the information provided in the tables. There are seemingly countless libraries available for C++ that are as compatible as the one provided here.

## *Table 1: User accessible functionality*

| Function or Variable | Description |
|---|---|
| .n rows | These are going to be the number of rows. |
| .n cols | These are the number of columns. |
| .n elem | These will be the amount of elements inside the table. |
| (i) | These will help you to access the i-th element and will assume that you have a layout that is column by column. |

| Function or Variable | Description |
| --- | --- |
| (r, c) | This is going to allow you to access the element that is in row r as well as in column c. |
| [i] | This will be as per (i), but there won't be any bounds check. |
| A(r, c) | This will be as per (r, c) but there won't be any bounds check. |
| .memptr() | This will allow the system to obtain the raw memory pointer that goes to the element data. |
| .in range(r,c) | This will test whether the program will be able to access what is in row r and column c. |
| .reset() | This is going to reset the number of elements that you have to zero. |
| .copy size(A) | This will set the size of everything to be the same as matrix A. |
| .set size (rows, cols) | This is going to change up the size of your dimensions, without keeping the data. |

| Function or Variable | Description |
| --- | --- |
| .reshape(rows, cols) | This is going to change up the size of your dimensions, while also keeping the data in place. |
| .fill(k) | This will set all of the elements in the table to be equal to the value of k. |
| .ones(rows, cols) | This is going to set all of the elements to one. |
| .zeroes(rows, cols) | This is going to set all of the elements in the table to zero. |
| .randu(rows, cols) | This is going to set the table to be uniformly distributed based on random values. |
| .is empty() | This will test whether there are any elements or not. |
| .is finite() | This will test whether the elements in the table are finite. |
| .is square() | This will take a look at the matrix and see if it is square. |
| .is vec() | This will check to see if the matrix is a vector. |

| Function or Variable | Description |
| --- | --- |
| Iterators: | This is going to be the iterators that you need to access the elements. |
| .begin() | This is the iterator that will point to the first element. |
| End() | This is the iterator that will point to the end element. |
| .begin row() | This iterator is going to point to the first element that is in the row you specify. |
| .end row() | This iterator is going to point to the element that is just one past the row you specify. |
| .begin col () | This iterator is going to point to the one element that is past the column you specify. |
| .print(header) | This is going to print the elements out in a continuous stream, with an optional header. |
| .print trans(header) | This is going to print the transposed version into storage. |
| .save | This will store the matrix in the file that you choose. |

| Function or Variable | Description |
| --- | --- |
| .load | This will retrieve the matrix from the file where you stored it and can sometimes specify the format of storage. |
| .diag(k) | This will provide access to the k-th diagonal. |
| .row(i) | This will provide access to the row i. |
| .col(i) | This is going to provide access to the column i. |
| .rows(a,b) | This will allow you to have access to the matrix that spans from row a to b. |
| Submat(p,q,r,s) | This will allow you to have access to the submatrix that starts at (p, q) and then ends at (r,s). |
| .swap rows | This is going to swap around the contents of the chosen rows. |
| .insert rows | This is going to insert a copy of your chosen row into a new one. |
| Shed rows | This is going to remove the rows that you want. |

| Function or Variable | Description |
| --- | --- |
| .shed cols | This will allow you to remove the columns that you want. |

## *Table 2: Operations for overload*

| Function | Description |
| --- | --- |
| nv(X) | This is going to be the inverse of the square matrix X. |
| Pinv(X) | This is the inverse of the non-square matrix X. |
| Solve(A,B) | This is going to solve the system for AX = B, where the X value is unknown. |
| Syd(X) | This is going to be the singular value decomposition of X. |
| Eig sym(X) | This is the Eigen decomposition of the matrix X. |
| Princomm(X) | This is going to be the principal component analysis of X. |
| Qr(Q,R,X) QR | This is going to be the decomposition of the X value so that QR = X. |

# Table 3: Decomposition of the matrix

| Function | Description |
|---|---|
| Eve(rows, cols) | This is the matrix that has the elements along the main diagonal so they are set to one. |
| Ones(rows, cols) | This is going to set the matrix up to have the elements all be one. |
| Zeroes(rows, cols) | This is going to set the matrix to have all the elements be zero. |
| Randu(rows, cols) | This is when the matrix is going to distribute the values randomly inside. |
| Randn(rows, cols) | This matrix is going to assign random values from their normal distribution. |
| Linspace(start, end, n) | This is the vector of n elements that will linearly increase. |
| Repmat(A, p, q) | This is going to replicate what is in matrix A which will result in a "p by q" block of A. |

## Table 4: Generating the matrix

| Function | Description |
|---|---|
| Accu(A) | This is going to be the accumulation of all the elements of A. |
| As scalar(expression) | This is going to evaluate the expression that will result in a 1 by 1 matrix and then will convert the results into a scalar. |
| Det (A) | This is going to be the determinant of the square matrix of A. |
| Log det(x, sign, A) | This is going to log the determinant of the A matrix so that the determinant is an exp(x)* sign. |
| Norm dot(A,B) | This is going to provide the normalized version of dot(A,B). |
| Rank(A) | This is going to provide the rank of matrix A. |
| Trace(A) | This is going to be the sum of the diagonal elements inside the square matrix A. |

## Table 5: Functions for scalar values

| Function | Description |
|---|---|
| Max(a,dim) | This is going to find the maximum of each column and each row you specify. |
| Min(A, dim) | This is going to find the minimum of the rows and columns you specify. |
| Prod(A, dim) | This is going to find the product of the rows and columns you specify. |
| Sum(A, dim) | This is going to find the sum of the rows and columns you specify. |
| Mean(A, dim) | This is going to find the average of the columns and rows you specify. |
| Median(a, dim) | This is going to find the median of the rows and columns you specify. |
| Stddev(A, dim) | This one is going to find all the standard deviations of your rows and columns. |
| Var(a, dim) | This is going to find the standard variance of the rows and columns you specify. |

| Function | Description |
|---|---|
| Diagvec(A, k) | This is going to extract the k-th diagonal from the matrix A. |

## Table 6: Vector and scalar functions

| Function | Description |
|---|---|
| Conv(A,B) | This is the convolution of A and B, and will assume they are vectors. |
| Cross(A,B) | This is going to be the cross product of A and B and will assume they are 3D vectors. |
| Krop(A,B) | This is going to be the Kronecker tensor product of these values. |
| Find(A) | This is going to find the indices of elements that are non-zero. |
| flipIr(A) | This is going to flip the matrices left-right. |
| Flipud(A) | This is going to flip the matrices up-down. |
| Join rows(A, B) | This is going to append each of the B rows with the A row it matches with. |

| Function | Description |
| --- | --- |
| Join cols(A, B) | This is going to append each of the B columns to the A column it matches with. |
| Reshape() | This is going to copy the dimensions of A to the columns and rows you choose. |
| Conj(C) | This is going to be a conjugation of the C matrix. |
| Real(C) | This is going to extract out the real part of the C matrix. |
| Sort index (A) | This is going to generate a vector which will describe the order of the elements of A, assuming that A is a vector. |
| Strans(A) | This is going to be a simple transpose of the A matrix. |

If you are not incredibly satisfied with the library provided, feel free to look up others. Some other common C++ libraries include:

## General Purpose Libraries

- Boost
- Loki
- MiLi
- POCO
- STL
- STXXL (used for extra-large data sets)
- Qt
- ASL
- JUCE

## Audio

- FMOD
- Synthesis Toolkit

## Database

- SOCI
- OTL
- LMDB++

## Design

- Hypodermic

- PocoCapsule
- Wallaroo

## Documents

- LibreOffice API
- PoDoFo

## Graphics

- Allegro
- OGRE
- SFML

## Imaging

- Boost.GIL
- Clmg
- DevIL
- EasyBMP
- FreeImage
- ITK
- OpenCV

## Logging

- Boost.Log
- Log4cxx

- Pantheios

- ICE

**Mocking**

- Google Mock

- Hippo Mocks

- Turtle (for boost)

**Testing**

- Boost.Test

- Google Test

- UnitTest++

**Multimedia**

- Openframework

- Cinder

- SDL

**XML**

- Libxml2

- Pugixml

- RapidXml

- TinyXML

**Networking**

- ACE

- Xerces-C++

- Boost.Asio

Each of the provided libraries listed here is an excellent choice for working in the respective programming fields listed. I encourage you to utilize only the libraries that are pertinent to the field of study within C++ you wish to pursue. Excessive libraries can be an incredibly daunting amount of information to take in. You can always add more later on.

# 4. Capabilities of C++

There are a lot of capabilities that come with using C++. You will find that the system is capable of doing almost anything you can set your mind to, as long as you have the right code obviously. C++ can open up an enormous world of capabilities. Let's take a look at drawing a shape with some programming:

```
class Shape (

public

virtual ~Shape():

virtual void draw() const = o

//...

);

//...

Shape *s =getSomeShape(); //pick out the shape that you will use
and tell it to...

s->draw(); //---start working!
```

At this point, we haven't listed out the shape that we want to work with, but we are working on creating the code that will make the form and teach it to draw itself. So now we are going to need to take it a bit further and tell the program what we want to have done. Let's say that we would like to pick out a form that is rollable; this is what the code would need to have inside for this part:

```
class Rollable (

public:

virtual ~Rollable();

virtual void roll() = 0;

);
```

With a class that is rollable, you are working with an interface class because it is going to work just in the interface. With this instance, we are going to assume that all of the items that get put into the rollable class are going to be able to roll. You will be able to tell the system which items you would like to let roll and which ones are not allowed or able to roll based on their shapes.

In some cases, it is extremely difficult, if not impossible, to know whether or not an object has the required ability to perform the task asked of it. In these situations, it is necessary to perform what is called a "capability query." In C++, this is typically done through a "dynamic cast" between the unfamiliar code and the operating system.

A "dynamic cast" attempts a conversion across the entirety of a grading, instead of simply up or down.

60

Capability queries are rarely needed, and some programmers have a tendency to overuse them. It is important to use them only when no other approach is possible.

The major advantages, put simply, are as follows:

- C++ is Object Oriented.

- You are capable of writing a program on any operating system, this is called portability. It allows you to move the program from one platform to another.

- It is very efficient for general-purpose, low-level programming.

- It has a high level of abstraction.

- It is compatible with the C programming language.

- It follows three paradigms. Generic, Imperative and Object Oriented.

# 5. Limitations of C++

Although C++ is used widely in the programming world, it does have its critics and it certainly has its own set of limitations. The five most common issues most programmers have when dealing with C++ are:

- The sheer complexity of the large language.

- No module system.

- Lack of practical garbage collection.

- Slow compilation.

- Excessive error messages, especially from template programming.

The universal criticism that will be thrown to new C++ learners is that it takes years and years to learn a language fluently, and that's just what C++ is, a language. You should not expect to be able to write complicated programs right off the bat with C++ or any other programming language. Instead, think of it like learning a new human language; learn basic phrases and your technique will improve with each "conversation" you have with the computer. For many years, the critics of C++ have grown, and as a result, other programming languages have been favored such as Python, Java, JavaScript, C, Scala, Clojure, and Ruby, to name a few.

Each programming language has its own set of syntaxes used to command or activate a function.

Perhaps one can also say that the fundamental differences between the languages comes down to the compatibility with the particular software application and file type that it underwrites and supports. With that statement, it is still important to note that the reason why C++ is taught in universities today for young minds wanting to have a career in the field of computer science, is because this language is imperative as the common foundation for many popular programs being created. Developers commonly argue that learning this language and understanding its argument logic will help you learn other programming languages easier and write a more powerful and faster program. For example, the syntax used in Java and Python languages frequently originates from C++.

Another common issue is that C++ does not have an easy way to differentiate and separate parts of the code. Other popular languages typically have sets of alphanumeric characters and certain symbols that separate the program into smaller modules, making it easier to execute part of the program later if needed, however C++ is notoriously known to not have a standard way to break down into sections. C++ is so powerful because it allows you to program almost anything, including the fact that you will have to write the commands that will differentiate parts of the code, instead of using built-in module systems or separators. For this reason, C++ can often trigger an error just from missing a parenthesis or comma.

In the world of computer science, garbage collection is just like deleting the cached memory on your cellular phone.

Popular programming languages have pre-made programs that automatically searches and "collects" unused memory by either placing it in a dedicated area in the system or deleting the "garbage". C++ had been long criticized for lacking the garbage collection feature, which naturally allowed third-party vendors to provide the service as extensions, which meant more cost for whoever wants to use it and additional work to test and implement the feature.

Compiling can be thought of as translating one language to another, and it is often a required task to make multiple programs interoperable. C++ is considered to have a longer compilation time compared to other languages like Java and C#. Poor time performance is certainly a limitation. For instance, larger compilation jobs can take all night and you may need the task completed by the morning when the businesses open. Well-discussed causes for the slow compilation starts with how the header files are loaded and compiled multiple times, which could be in the thousands. Other reasons include how C++ scripts are written in a way that object files must be processed one by one, dependent sequentially, and multiple lines cannot be processed in parallel.

Once the script's objects, semantic, and syntactic foundations are identified, the complex syntax is usually parsed slower in C++ than in other languages, usually because the entire code section preceding it inserts the context on how the syntaxes are supposed to be handled. Other than increasing the RAM and CPUs, programmers can invest time into utilizing precompiled headers and tools that can allow it to simultaneously run multiple compilations when wanting to improve the performance solely inside the code.

Precompiled headers are commonly used for large sections of the script that the programmers know have the identical headers. You probably sense by now that most of the C++ limitations stem from the complexity of the language syntax itself. This unleashes more unlimited potential rather than limitations. However, you will quickly notice that the excessive error messages, especially from template programming, is unavoidable.

With C++, you will find redundancy is one of your biggest issues. When dealing with the frustration of learning to write code, you will need to execute, absolutely perfectly, the same line over and over and (one more time) over again. Do not be discouraged by this. Redundant repetition is the only way to write in C++ and it is what is necessary to accomplish your goals to be a programmer. The critics will talk, but you should let your coding speak for you.

Efficiency is the only criticism you should pay any mind to, if your program isn't efficient, then it is simply not going to be useful to you. As you can probably tell, C++ is not perfect. Like many languages, its flaws can be picked apart and can seem daunting. That being said, the advantages far outweigh the disadvantages.

# 6. Practical Application of C++

Whats are the real-life applications of C++ and its benefit to advance in your job prospects? Of course, exposure to multiple programming languages will open more doors to career choices, but that does not correlate to an increase in job security. C++ is intricate to learn, but it is extensively used and well alive today.

Just as an introduction of how versatile C++ is, the language is dominantly used in the following parts of the modern world:

- In the infrastructure of large-scale office applications targeted to enterprises.

- In the development of hardware and core software systems such as drivers for devices, operating systems, graphics processing, database engines, user-interfaces, and desktop applications.

- Performance intensive tasks like processing audio, as well as image compilations.

- As the tool to maintain legacy systems due to its long-lived adaptation.

- Console and computer gaming industries.

- Embedded systems and desktop software for the telecommunication sector.

- Analysis and operating applications for banking and financial institutions.

- Server applications for the defense and security industry.

- Engineering CAD and CAM applications.

- Scientific computing.

If your interest in programming is predominantly web-based, then note that applications running the web browsers are typically not written in C++, but rather written in JavaScript. The same can be noted for applications that monopolize the programming language to a brand of products, such as the ABAP language for a large commercial software called SAP and Objective-C for Apple products. Despite this, if a software using C++ was to integrate with the web browser or brand-specific applications, then C++ is the main language used in making multiple platforms interoperate.

Your dedication to learn C++ will surely reward you for many decades to come as a developer and programmer in a multitude of industries and career levels.

# 7. Making Your First C++ Program

Let's get started on writing your first program. It is recommended that you invest in tools like the Integrated Development Environments (IDE) that can help you program more simply. Each one can provide you great features to a well-organized and productive environment to program away. Popular productivity features in these tools include automatic highlighting of syntaxes, checking of syntax and logic errors, code previewing, tabbed interfaces, automatic file comparison, debugging, built-in compilers, and support for multiple languages.

As you become more familiar with programming and have specific programming goals, you can shop around for an IDE that will best serve your needs. Some IDE's can help you beyond programming. For instance, some have a built-in feature to manage projects against timelines, share testing progress with others, and search open source codes that are already written and openly shared by others. For enthusiastic beginners, the best part of the IDE software listed below is that most are free of cost.

Code editing IDE's recommended for beginner C++ programmers, are any of the following:

- Eclipse
- ConTEXT
- CodeLite
- Visual Studio
- NetBeans
- Code Blocks
- Dev-C
- Devpad
- Notepad++
- Ultimate++
- NinjaI
- ChSciTE
- NewbieIDE
- AEdiX
- Ynote Classic
- Crimson Editor
- Textplorer
- QT Creator
- SkyIDE
- Falcon C++
- PSPad Editor
- WxDev-C
- C.vim
- Sally
- Quincy
- Relo
- cIDEE
- Bonfire Studio
- Geany
- Simpedit
- Notemaster

In this section, you will be learning how to write a simple C++ program. Below is an open-source program that will quickly and easily convert temperatures from Celsius to Fahrenheit. These are the codes needed to get started.

## Example 22: The following program is used to showcase how you can design your first C++ program.

```cpp
#include <iostream>
#include <conio.h>

using namespace std;

int main()
{
// This is my first program
    float c, f;

    cout<<"Welcome, this program converts Celsius to Fahrenheit"<<endl;
    cout<< "Enter the degree in Celsius:"<<endl;

    cin>>c;
    f=c*1.8+32;

    cout<<"The degree in Fahrenheit is "<<f;
    getch();

return 0;
}
```

The output of the above program will be as follows. The program will ask the user for an input, so if you enter the value input of 34 , you will get the below output:

**Welcome, this program converts Celsius to**

**Fahrenheit**

**Enter the degree in Celsius:**

34

34

**The degree in Fahrenheit is 93.2**

Next, I will explain what the different blocks of code are:

### 1) #include

These lines add the base files. Any line starting with the # symbol is called the preprocessor directive and it instructs what header standard is used to read and compile the rest of the code. In this case, the #include refers to a preprocessor directive referred to as the <iostream.h> header, which applies the standard C++ input and output rules.

### 2) Namespace

Next we use the namespace std. This is so that when we use the normal statements of cout and cin , we don't need to add the prefix as std::cout and std::cin.

### 3) main()

This calls the main function. A function is made up of pre-built codes. This one is used to execute the start of all C++ programs.

### 4) float c, f;

This declares that "c" and "f" are float. In this case, representing "Celsius" and "Fahrenheit" respectively.

## 5) cout<<"...";

This line "prints", which in the world of C++, it means to display the texts on the screen for the user as is. In other words, when quotation marks surround texts, the quoted text will appear for the user of the program on the screen, exactly as it is written.

## 6) cin>>c:

This line defines an input value of "c"

## 7) f=c*1.8+32;

This line defines an input value of "f"

## 8) cout<<" The degree in Fahrenheit is" <<f;

This line again prints the texts and displays the value of "f". Instead of literally displaying the alphabet "f", the calculated value from line 9 will display since quotation marks did not surround it.

## 9) getch();

This line stops the program for one second.

## 10) return 0;

This line signifies the end of the program.

## 11) }

This line signifies the end of the program's code.


Congratulations on writing and understanding your first C++ program.

Next, you will see several other simple programs to show you how the preprocessor directives, function calls, and value definitions can vary.

## Example 23: The following program is used to return the current date and time for the user.

```
#include <time.h>
#include<stdio.h>
#include<string>
#include<iostream>

//make the date and time show up as year, month, day, hour,
minute, second
const std::string ShowCurrentDateTime(){

  time_t    now = time(0);
  struct tm  tstruct;
  char      buf[80];
  tstruct = *localtime(&now);

  strftime(buf, sizeof(buf), "%Y-%m-%d.%X", &tstruct);

  return buf;
}

int main() {
  std::cout << " ShowCurrentDateTime ()=" <<
ShowCurrentDateTime () << std::endl;
  getchar();  // wait for keyboard input

}
```

With this program, the output will return the following value for January, 2nd 2017 at 1pm 14 minutes 59 seconds:

**ShowCurrentDateTime ()=2017-01-02.13:14:59**

## *Example 24: The following program is used to detect a certain alphanumeric character and replace it with another. In this case, the program will look for the character strings "fun" and replace it with "very fun".*

```
#include <algorithm>
#include <iostream>
#include <string>

using namespace std;

int main()

  {

  string s = "C++ is fun to learn.";

  replace( s.begin(), s.end(), 'fun', 'very fun' );

  cout << s << endl;

  return 0;

  }
```

This program's output will return this value:

**"C++ is very fun to learn."**

## Example 25: The following program that will allow you to play the simple game, Hangman.

```cpp
#include<iostream>
#include<conio.h>
#include <cstring>


using namespace std;

int main()
{
    int lifes=0;
    char letter;
    int none;
    char wordtoguess[50]={0};
    char guessedword[50]={0};

    cout<<"Type out a word to play Hangman: "<<endl;
    cin>> wordtoguess;

    while ( lifes <=5 && strcmp(guessedword, wordtoguess) != 0)

    {
        none=0;
        cout<<endl<<"Please guess a letter: ";
        cin>>letter;

        for(int n=0; n<50; n++) {

            if(wordtoguess [n] == letter) {
                guessedword [n]= wordtoguess [n];
                none=1; } }

        if(none<1) {
```

```
        lifes=lifes+1;
        cout<<"Try once more!"<<endl; }
    }

    if (lifes>5) {
        cout<<endl<<"You lose!"; }
    else {
        cout<<endl<<"You win!"; }

    getch();
    return 0;
}
```

When you compile the above Hangman code, the output will ask you for a single word that will be assigned as the value "wordtoguess":

**Type out a word to play Hangman:**

Then when the codes are executed, the output will ask the user for the "guessedword":

**Please guess a letter:**

Depending on the guessed word containing the alphanumeric character in the "wordtoguess", the code will return:

**You lose!** or **You win!**

In the next chapters, you will learn how to avoid bugs and to be aware of hacking vulnerability in your codes.

# 8. How to Avoid Adding Bugs to Your Programs

Programming will come with more than its fair share of frustrations. At the top of the list of frustrations will be bugs in your program. A bug in the software is basically an error in the system that causes an incorrect or unexpected result. Bugs can be divided into syntax bugs and logic bugs. Syntax bugs are usually detected by the compiler and are easy to fix. Logic bugs are detected by analyzing the program output and are harder to find.

Warnings and error messages will be extremely common occurrences in any programming language. It's all part of the job, or so they say. In this chapter, I will teach you how to minimize bugs in your programs.

## 8.1 Enabling Warning and Error Messages

The syntax used in C++ will allow the user to do an incredible amount of error checking. When the compiler encounters a code it cannot read, it will be forced to push back an error message to the programmer. The compiler will then attempt to sync with the next statement provided in the code, however, it will not attempt to create a usable program.

Consider these error messages to be significant, do not disable your warning and error messages simply because they may seem annoying. Ignoring a problem does not make it go away. Always enable your syntax check mode in your compiler.

All of that being said, do not start to debug your code until you understand all of the warnings or errors created during compilation. Adopt a clear and consistent coding style to help you be able to pick out certain errors within a line of code and ultimately correct them.

## 8.2 Developing Consistent Coding

Keeping your coding consistent can be an extremely daunting task, especially when dealing with more complex programs. But as your programs become more and more complex, it is of the utmost importance to keep your coding even more consistent than if you were developing a simple program like the ones we have gone over in this book.

Well-structured code will make your program more readable and will also inherently result in fewer coding mistakes when all is said and done. It will allow you to differentiate the names of the classes, objects, and functions more easily. It will make naming objects and identifying them a simple task. It will also help identify blocks of code.

To do this, you will need to create a standard header for your module that will give you information about the functions and classes contained therein. You can utilize code::blocks to maintain your coding style for you by selecting the "source formatter" in the settings of your code editor.

## 8.3 Single Step Every Coding Path Twice

It is imperative for a programmer to understand exactly what the program being created is doing. This may sound like an obvious statement, but this should be taken quite literally. You should go through each individual line of code, understand its function, and be certain that it will be executed appropriately for the program being developed. This ensures familiarity when all of the functions are put together to create the program. Bugs will be much simpler to fix when the function in question has been looked over a few times before.

## 8.4 Manage Your Program Systematically

Programmers should assign and free memory at the same level. If a function of a member assigns a block of memory that is subsequently returned to the caller, you should see a member function that returns the memory again. You should not be required to have the parent function release the memory. This will reduce the probability of running into major memory leaks, especially when working with larger programs.

## 8.5 Exception Mechanisms

A good programmer will utilize exceptions in an attempt to handle the errors that show up. The exception mechanism is created to deal with errors more expediently. Throwing an error indicator is preferable to returning an error flag. As a result, your code will be simpler to read, write, and maintain.

## 8.6 Create Destructors for Your Class

Do this when the constructor places resources, that should be brought back when the object is being canceled. Remember to state your destructor as virtual when you know that the class is likely to be inherited by a subclass.

## 8.7 Multiple Inheritance

A programmer should try to avoid multiple inheritances. Similar to the problems created with overloading, multiple inheritances will add a whole new level of complexity that is unnecessary for a beginner. Most programs can be described with a single inheritance. However, as your skill with C++ progresses, experiment by setting up hierarchies with multiple inheritances. So when the rare occasion comes when you need to use multiple inheritances, you will be prepared.

# 9. How to Avoid Being Hacked

Although none of the programs we make in this book would ever be considered for an attack by a hacker, once you get into the real world of programming as it pertains to the workplace, you'll find hackers are a very dangerous part of the job. While writing hacker proof code in C++ is most likely impossible, we can examine the attacks used by hackers to expose weaknesses and strengthen our own programs. Hackers tend to find a way around almost any problem, so countering an attack is a hard task indeed. Let's look at a few of the reasons your program may be hacked.

In the best case scenario, a hacker may attempt to shut down your program by overflowing it. This is most commonly done because the hacker does not like the organization for which the program has been written, it can cost the business a lot of money in lost revenue for the time that the program in question is down. It can also cost the company customers, who may become frustrated because they are unable to access the information they require.

In the worst case scenario, a hacker will attempt to attain client or account information. This is usually done for two reasons. Less common is to hold the information hostage in exchange for a reward.

The more common reason for these attacks is to access account information from say, a bank, and transfer funds from a large account to their own accounts. These attacks are incredibly hard to trace. It is in the best interest of the programmer to create a program that cannot be accessed easily from the outside.

The most common attack programmers using C++ will encounter is a SQL injection. This takes an extreme amount of guess work from the hacker. Unfortunately for the programmer, hackers have plenty of time to do guess work and usually have extensive knowledge of how code is written to make educated guesses. As this book is covering C++ and not SQL, I will not delve too deep into how that works.

It is important to know however, that the best way to avoid having your program hacked is to create a system of formal verifications. That is, do not allow your code to be accessed with questions, only facts. Formal verification is the process of proving or disproving the accuracy of applied algorithms in a system with certain formal specifications. This will greatly limit the amount of guesswork the hacker will be able to do. It will force back inconsistent error messages to the hacker attempting to infiltrate your program and make it nearly impossible for them to attain any useful information.

Hacking is a serious part of the programming world. Hackers have found this to be a profitable field, because they are able to get hold of valuable information that could be worth a lot of money to the right people. This is why it is so important to make sure that your computer is as safe as possible. There are always hackers out there who could take your information. If you are not careful with how you store your data or what links you click on, you will find that your information could be vulnerable to attack.

There are a few techniques to protect yourself and your program from possible hackers:

## *Be careful with links*

Links are often your worst enemy when it comes to your computer's safety. If you click on a link that you aren't sure about, especially when it comes via email, you could be vulnerable to an attack. If you get an email requesting you to click on a link, rather go to your browser and type in the address or search for the company to get their legitimate website. This ensures that you end up at the right site, rather than one that may be a fake. Also never provide your information over an email.

## *Have some protection in place*

Whether you are working on an important project or not, you should have some kind of protection in place for your computer. There is always the risk of attacks online, through a website, or your network. Make sure that you have at least a good anti-virus and firewall in place.

## *Don't go to a website you don't trust*

Always be careful with the websites you visit. Hackers could place ads on sites that look legitimate, but in reality are fishing for your info. Be especially careful on sites with download links. You should always be on alert when you are asked for your personal details, even on authentic sites.

A very important tip is to look for the site authentication when making online purchases. It is usually represented with a padlock icon next to the website address. Clicking the icon should provide details about the site you are currently on and if your connection is secure.

## Make strong passwords

Be careful with the passwords that you use. Pick something that is a complex combination of random characters (if possible) and never use the same password for more than one account. That way if one of your accounts has been compromised, the hacker wouldn't have access to the rest of your accounts.

A fellow developer I knew had a 20 digit computer password, made up of random characters. He would then add two random characters every year and commit the entire thing to memory. Naturally this is a bit on the extreme side, but gives you an idea of what some people would do to protect their information.

## Always be on the lookout

The moment that you assume that no one is going to attack your computer, is when you are most vulnerable. It is always best to assume the worst and that you could be under attack, and just take the extra precautions to protect your information.

## Learn some basic hacking techniques

While this guidebook is not going to go into detail about how to hack, learning a few hacking techniques can help. This is going to allow you to identify some of the vulnerabilities in your system so that you can fix them.

You never know when your system could be the next to be under attack. Whether you are creating new code for your job, or just want to keep your personal information safe, it is a good idea to be vigilant and take precautionary measures.

# 10. Glossary of Terms

There are a lot of terms that have come up in this guidebook. Some of them are rather easy to figure out and have been explained along the way, but others may be a bit confusing still. Here is a small list to help you get started and to make it easier to get through this coding language as a beginner.

## Abstract class

This is a class that has been designated to be a base class for other classes and contains any pure virtual functions.

## Address

Every variable or object in a program is located at a particular address in a computer's memory. Addresses can be assigned to pointers which are then used to refer to that memory location.

## Allocation

This refers to the process of manually allocating memory space to an object.

## Application

An application program is a collection of statements designed to serve a common purpose for an end user.

## Argument

This is a section of data that is passed into a function or program. Also known as a parameter.

## Array

An array is a data structure that allows storage and fast access to a collection of data values. The stored values are all of the same data type, such as an array of integers or an array of characters.

## Assignment

The assignment statement is the process of giving a value to a variable or object.

## Base class

A base class can be seen as a parent class for other classes. It is used to create or derive other classes. These derived classes inherit their data and behavior from the base class. For example, if "fruit" is a base class then "apples" and "oranges" would be derived classes.

## Bit

This is the smallest unit of data that can be manipulated in a computer. It has a binary value of 0 or 1. Memory bits are combined to form bytes.

## Boolean

This is a data type that has only two values, "true" and "false". It provides a yes/no outcome to logic and Boolean algebra statements.

## Break

A break statement is used to exit a loop. When the break statement is encountered in a loop, the program exits the loop and continues with the next statement that follows the loop. An example is to use a break within an if statement, that exits the loop once a condition is met.

## Breakpoint

A breakpoint temporarily halts the execution of the program during a debugging session. It is then possible to examine the contents of the memory and variables. A breakpoint does not cancel program execution, it merely "pauses" it.

## Bug

A software bug is an error in a program that causes an incorrect or unexpected result. Bugs can be divided into syntax bugs and logic bugs. Syntax bugs are usually detected by the compiler and are easy to fix. Logic bugs are detected by analyzing the program output and are harder to find.

## Byte

A byte is a unit of data consisting of eight bits, which a computer typically groups as one logical unit.

## Class

A class is a user-defined data structure that describes one or more objects. It can be seen as the blueprint for creating specific objects in a program. Access to a class can be set as private, public or protected. A class allows variables to be isolated from other parts of the program.

## Comments

Comments are ignored by the compiler. They increase the readability of code by adding notes for future reference.

## Compiler

A compiler is a program that converts text source code into a binary or executable format, which is machine readable and can be run by a computer.

## Concatenation

This refers to the joining two strings, by joining the start of the second string to the end of the first.

## Constructor

A constructor is a member function that initializes an object. It is called automatically. If no constructors are defined, such as a parameterized constructor, then the compiler will use the default constructor.

## Container

This is a type of class that holds objects and provides access to them. Examples would be lists and strings.

## Data structure

This refers to the way data is grouped together under one name. It is similar to an array, but stored values can be of different types. Examples are lists, stacks, queues and trees.

## Debugger

A debugger is a tool used to test and debug a program. It is able to step through the execution of a program to locate and identify code errors.

## Declaration

This refers to declaring an object to the compiler. All variables are declared by stating the name and data type of the variable. This way the compiler knows how to handle the variable and how much storage space to allocate.

## Destructor

The destructor is a member function that is, in a way, the opposite of the "constructor" function. It is automatically executed during the closing or deletion of an object. Its main function is releasing memory and network resources allocated to the object.

## Encapsulation

Encapsulation is the bundling of data along with the functions that manipulate that data together. It is a method of hiding the internal parts of an object to protect the object's integrity. This method is also said to reduce complexity.

## Exception handling

An exception is another name for an error. Exceptions can occur due to a problem with the program design or lack of system resources. Exception handling is the process of identifying and dealing with errors or exceptions. C++ uses catch clauses and try blocks as part of its exception handling.

## Expression

An expression is simply a statement that resolves to a value.

## Function

A function is a block of code that accomplishes a specific task. C++ has numerous functions contained in its library that can be called. Every program must have at least one function, being the "main" function.

## Global variable

A global variable's scope is defined to the entire program. It can thus be accessed from all parts of a program.

## Handle

A handle is a reference to a specific entity or resource. A handle can be used without much knowledge about the resource it identifies. An example would be a pointer that references the address of an object in memory.

## Hash

A hash is a data structure that stores pairs of keys and values. A value can then be inserted or retrieved based on its key.

## Inheritance

Inheritance is the process where a derived class inherits properties and behaviors from a base class.

## Initialization

This is the process where an object or variable is assigned a value at their point of creation.

## Inline function

This is a C++ feature that can improve compile time at the cost of memory. An inline function acts as a placeholder. When the "inline" keyword is used, the compiler will place a copy of the code of that function at each instance where the function is called. This saves time required to call the function.

## Integral type

Integral type refers to "integer" types or whole numbers. Examples are bool, char, int, long and short.

## Keyword

Keywords are words that are reserved for a special purpose in a programming language. They are used to declare properties of an object, declare object types, and create program structures.

## Library

A library is a set of prewritten code that a programmer can call upon. It is code written usually by someone else and can be used legally within a program. Two general types exist, static and dynamic. A static library essentially forms part of program by taking copies of the code and adding it to the program. A dynamic library or shared library's code is only referenced when used.

## Loop

A loop is a statement that, as the name suggests, loops repeatedly. It executes the specified instructions continually until a certain condition is met. That condition could be (for example) to run the statement 10 times or to run the statement until a "true" value is received.

## Main

Every program must have a single main function. Program execution begins with the first main statement.

## Memory leak

A memory leak occurs when memory is not released from a program and impairs performance. Memory is allocated to objects during a program's execution. When the object is no longer in use, the memory should be released. When this is not done, it can unnecessarily occupy the computer's memory and affect performance.

## Name

A name is merely an identifier. It designates functions, members, objects, templates and labels.

## Nested class

This is a class that is enclosed within another class. The nested class is a member of the enclosing class.

## New

This keyword is used to allocate memory to objects. Memory can be allocated to a single object when it is initialized, or a block of memory can be allocated to more than one object at a time. The keyword also returns the address of the allocated memory.

## Null

A special reserved value that represents a null pointer. All pointer types have this reserved value and is essentially used when a pointer is not pointing anywhere.

## Object

An object refers to an instance of a class. It can be a function, method, variable or data structure.

## Operator

An operator is a symbol that instructs the program to perform a mathematical or logical operation on two terms and produce a result. Examples of operators are arithmetic (+ - * /), relational (== < >) and logical (&& !).

## Parameter

A parameter is a variable in a program that refers to a piece of data used as an input into a function or subroutine.

## Parsing

In simple terms, this is the process where a program or block of data is broken down into smaller components to be processed. In programming, code is broken down into tokens, whereby a parser builds a data structure based on the tokens. This data structure is then used by a compiler to create a program.

## Pointer

Pointers are used to reference the address of an object that has been stored in the computer's memory. They can also be used to pass arguments to functions.

## Prefix

This refers to operators that appear before their operands. Operands are the data to be manipulated.

## Preprocessor

The preprocessor is a program runs prior to another program. The outputs from the preprocessor are used as inputs for a subsequent program.

## Private

This is a keyword that declares a class member's access as private. The member can then only be accessed by function within the class and not from other classes or subclasses.

## Programming environment

This refers to the software tools used in developing programs, including a text editor, compiler, browser and interpreter.

## Public

This is a keyword that declares a class member's access as public. The member has no access restrictions and can be accessed by any class.

## Queue

A queue in programming, functions the same as a queue in the real world. It is a data structure that supports first in first out (FIFO) processing. Objects are processed in the order they appear in the queue.

## Recursion

Recursion is a tool used to have a function call on itself. The code it usually iterative with a different argument added, in order for the function to not call itself infinitely.

## Reference

References are a feature of C++ and refer to an alias or alternative name for a variable. A reference is used to pass a variable to a function, without copying the variable. It instead references back to the variable's memory.

## Source code

Source code is the human-readable instructions written by the programmer, which is turned into machine-readable form by a compiler.

## Stack

A stack is similar to a queue, but functions on the last in first out (LIFO) principle. Objects that were added last are processed first, similar to a stack of dishes being cleaned.

## Statement

A statement is the smallest standalone element of a program. It is a command given to the computer. In C++, statements end in a semicolon.

## String

A string is a sequence of text characters and always ends in a null character (\0). C++ has numerous built-in functions to manipulate strings, such as concatenate, search and extract.

## Syntax

Syntax is the rules that govern how functions, comments and whitespaces are to be structured to form a program.

## Template

This forms the basis of generic programming and allows for creating a generic class or function. The C++ library provides templates to define functions and classes.

## Tree

A tree is a type of data structure used for storing and retrieving data. In a tree structure, each module consists of a single parent with multiple children.

## Try block & Catch clause

C++ utilizes try blocks and catch clauses in exception handling. A try block contains a section or block of code that may cause an exception. A try block is mostly followed by a catch clause, which catches and handles the exception if it occurs.

## Type checking

Type checking is a method that ensures "type" programming errors are identified and reported. A type checker confirms that the type of a variable, array, list or constant matches what is expected of it. For example if the variable type is Integer, then the value passed should be Integer.

## Type conversion

Type conversion refers to the conversion of an entity from one data type to another. This can be done automatically, known as implicit conversion, or through the type cast operator, known as explicit conversion.

## Unary operator

These are operators that require only one operand. They operate on the object for which they are called and are usually placed before the object. Examples are increment (++), decrement (--) and logical not (!) operators.

## Union

This is a special data type that allows different data types to be stored in the same memory location at different times. Space is allocated based on the largest object and only one member can contain a value at a specific point in time.

## Variable

A variable is an object of a specified type, which contains a known or unknown quantity of information.

## White space

White space is used to make code easier to read for the programmer. It includes blank spaces, blank lines and tabs. These white spaces are ignored by the program compiler.

# Conclusion

You have made it to the end of the first book in our Step-By-Step C++ series. If you enjoyed getting started with C++, there is so much more to learn and do with this wonderful language. Be sure to continue your journey with the second book in the series, *C++: A Detailed Approach to Practical Coding*.

C++ is a valuable programming language with a large array of uses. It is practical, efficient, and most importantly, easily modified. It will be your greatest asset and your best reference point for your future in programming. If you can think it, you can create it. Don't be afraid to try something new.

Good luck and happy programming!

# About the Author

Nathan Clark is an expert programmer with nearly 20 years of experience in the software industry.

With a master's degree from MIT, he has worked for some of the leading software companies in the United States and built up extensive knowledge of software design and development.

Nathan and his wife, Sarah, started their own development firm in 2009 to be able to take on more challenging and creative projects. Today they assist high-caliber clients from all over the world.

Nathan enjoys sharing his programming knowledge through his book series, developing innovative software solutions for their clients and watching classic sci-fi movies in his free time.